SAYINGS and PHRASES

It's a Long Shot!

(And Other Strange Sayings)

written by Cynthia Amoroso ★ illustrated by Mernie Gallagher-Cole

ABOUT THE AUTHOR

As a high school English teacher and as an elementary teacher, Cynthia Amoroso has shared her love of language with students. She has always been fascinated with idioms and figures of speech. Today Cynthia is a school district administrator in Minnesota. She has two daughters who also share her love of language through reading, writing, and talking!

ABOUT THE ILLUSTRATOR

Mernie Gallagher-Cole lives in Pennsylvania with her husband and two children. She uses sayings and phrases like the ones in this book every day. She has illustrated many children's books, including *Messy Molly* and *Día De Los Muertos* for The Child's World®.

The Child's World®

Published by The Child's World®
1980 Lookout Drive • Mankato, MN 56003-1705
800-599-READ • www.childsworld.com

ACKNOWLEDGMENTS
The Child's World®: Mary Berendes, Publishing Director

The Design Lab: Kathleen Petelinsek, Design and Page Production

LIBRARY OF CONGRESS CATALOGING-IN-PUBLICATION DATA
Amoroso, Cynthia.
 It's a long shot!: (and other strange sayings) / by Cynthia Amoroso ; illustrated by Mernie Gallagher-Cole.
    p. cm.
 ISBN 978-1-60253-683-8 (library bound: alk. paper)
1. English language—Idioms—Juvenile literature.
2. Figures of speech—Juvenile literature. 3. Clichés—Juvenile literature. I. Gallagher-Cole, Mernie. II. Title.
 PE1460.A585 2011
 428.1—dc22   2010042740

Printed in the United States of America
Mankato, MN
December, 2010
PA02067

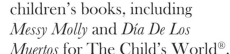

People use idioms *(ID-ee-umz) every day. These are sayings and phrases with meanings that are different from the actual words. Some idioms seem silly. Many of them don't make much sense . . . at first.*

This book will help you understand some of the most common idioms. It will tell you how you might hear a saying or phrase. It will tell you what the saying really means. All of these sayings and short phrases—even the silly ones—are an important part of our language!

TABLE *of* CONTENTS

Better late than never

Emmett looked at the parking lot. The game started ten minutes ago. Dad told him he was coming tonight. Emmett would be up to bat soon.

"Hey, buddy!" yelled Dad as he trotted toward the field.

"I thought you weren't going to make it," said Emmett.

"Better late than never!" said Dad. "Traffic was terrible. I'm lucky I got here at all!"

MEANING: To be late is better than not coming at all

The buck stops here

The softball team was getting new uniforms. People had a lot of different ideas about what the uniforms should look like.

"Who makes the final decision?" asked Anthony.

"I do," said the coach. "I'm always happy to hear people's ideas, but somebody has to make the final choice. That's me—the buck stops here."

MEANING: When someone takes full responsibility for a situation or a decision

4

Chicken out

Nate stood on the dock and looked at the lake. He was nervous. Today, he was going to try wakeboarding for the first time.

His cousin Jillian grinned at him. "What's the matter, Nate? Afraid?"

That was enough to get Nate going! The next thing he knew, he was zipping through the water.

"Whoo!" Nate hollered to Jillian when he was done. "That was fun! And I bet you thought I was going to chicken out."

MEANING: To be afraid of something; to choose not to do something because of fear

Close call

Kelsey and her dad were painting the living room. They spread out plastic sheets to protect the furniture and floor. Kelsey opened a new can of paint and stirred it. She started to carry it over to where they were working. Just then, her toe caught on the edge of a plastic sheet. Luckily, she didn't fall—or drop the paint.

"Whew!" she said to her dad. "That was a really close call!"

MEANING: When something almost happens

Don't count your chickens before they're hatched

Zack and his brother Evan were playing. Their dad was reading a book nearby.

"You know that big tank we saw in the store?" said Zack. "I'm going to buy it. I'm saving up for it."

"Doesn't it cost a lot of money?" asked Evan.

"Sure," Zack said, "but I can make a lot of money weeding Mr. Kiefer's yard this weekend."

"Hold on," said Dad. "You haven't even talked to him about that yet. Don't count your chickens before they're hatched!"

MEANING: Don't make plans based on something that hasn't happened yet

False alarm

"Oh no!" said Corey. "I think I left my sunglasses at the fair!"

"Do you have any idea where?" asked Mom. "We went to a lot of places."

Corey thought hard. "I remember having them at the giant slide. I think I took them off before I went on the roller coaster."

Just then Corey looked down. His sunglasses were on the floor of the car.

"Oops! False alarm!" he said. "They're right here."

MEANING: To find out that something you thought was a problem is not a problem

Food for thought

Mrs. Welch's history class had just finished listening to a guest speaker. The speaker was a doctor who worked in some of the poorest regions in the world. Mrs. Welch was asking the students what they had learned.

"I didn't know so many people don't have clean water to drink!" said Chandra. "I liked that he told us how we can get involved, too."

"He had some great ideas," agreed Mrs. Welch. "It's really food for thought, isn't it?"

MEANING: Something to think about; ideas; information that may help you make a decision

Get to the bottom of it

Dad and Mariah were weeding the garden. Mom came out with some cold lemonade.

"How does it look?" she asked. "Did you figure out what's been eating the lettuce?"

"It must be a rabbit," said Mariah. "We just can't figure out how it's getting in."

"Don't worry," Dad said. "It's a mystery, but we'll get to the bottom of it!"

MEANING: To solve a problem; to figure something out; to get needed information

Go against the grain

Grandpa was thinking about buying another car. He and his grandsons were talking about what kind he should get.

Robbie said, "I think you should buy something new."

"Yeah," Nick agreed, "something nice and fast." He pointed to a picture of a sporty red convertible.

Grandpa laughed. "Did you see how much that car costs? I'm a sensible guy. I don't want to spend that much for a car. That would really go against the grain for me!"

MEANING: To do something against your nature or preferences; to act differently from the majority

Hang in there

Dave had a broken foot. His friends were out riding bikes, but all he could do was sit at home. He propped his foot on a stool and gave a long sigh.

"What's the matter?" asked his dad.

"I'm really tired of this," Dave said. "I'm tired of sitting around."

"Hang in there, buddy," Dad replied. "One more week and you'll be out of that cast."

MEANING: To keep trying even when you are tired or frustrated; to stay positive

Hit the sack

Kyra and her family were camping. They were sitting around the campfire, roasting marshmallows, and watching the flames.

"Wow!" her dad said, looking at his watch. "I didn't know it was this late. We have to leave pretty early tomorrow. Let's put out the fire. We'd better hit the sack."

MEANING: Go to bed

In over his head

Jonah loved to take things apart and figure out how they worked. He was pretty good at putting them back together, too. He had taken his bike apart, trying to fix the gears. Now he couldn't figure out how to get everything back where it belonged.

Jonah's mom saw him sitting by the pieces, looking discouraged.

"Uh-oh," she said to Dad. "We better go help. I think he's in over his head."

MEANING: Trying to do something that is more than you can handle

It's a long shot

Dustin wanted to do something fun before summer ended.

"I have an idea," said Dustin to his brother Jake. "Let's ask Mom if we can go camping this weekend. We haven't done that for a long time."

"Great idea!" said Jake. "But I think Mom might have other plans."

"Well, I'm going to ask her anyway," Dustin said. "It's a long shot, but it's worth a try!"

MEANING: When there is little chance of something happening; when something is unlikely

Neat as a pin

Caroline's family was moving. They packed and moved boxes all day. Other people helped, too. Caroline's Aunt Jenna did everything from wrapping glasses to sweeping the floor. At the end of the day, Caroline and her mom looked up. Aunt Jenna was standing there in her perfectly white shirt and shorts.

"Look at you!" exclaimed Mom. "How do you do that? We're all wrinkled and dirty, and you look neat as a pin!"

MEANING: Very clean

No love lost

Jude liked to visit his grandpa. His grandpa was really nice. He met grandpa's neighbors, and they seemed really nice, too. That's why he was surprised when two of the neighbors walked past each other without saying hello.

"Why don't they talk to each other?" Jude asked his grandpa.

"It's pretty silly, really," Grandpa said. "A long time ago they had an argument, and they never got over it. They're good people, but there's no love lost between them, that's for sure!"

MEANING: When people don't like each other

15

Off the beaten path

Mr. Riley just returned from London. He showed some great pictures to his fifth grade class. They saw everything from dungeons to trains, and funny little buildings that looked really old.

"How did you find all those places?" asked Parker.

"My friend has lived in London for years," Mr. Riley replied. "He loves to explore, and he knows his way around. He takes me to places that are really off the beaten path!"

MEANING: Different or unusual; also, an uncommon destination or route

Out of sorts

Everything Brandon did seemed to make his sister Regan mad. She didn't have one nice thing to say to him.

"What's wrong with Regan?" Brandon asked his mom. "She's being really grumpy with me. I didn't even do anything!"

"She tired, and she thinks she might be coming down with a cold," Mom answered. "It's nothing serious—she's just feeling out of sorts."

MEANING: In a bad mood; not feeling well; not feeling like you normally do

Pick your brain

Faith was stumped. She needed to start her science fair project, but she didn't have any good ideas. She called up her friend Stephanie and explained the problem.

"Steph, you always have great ideas for projects," Faith said. "I need to come up with a really good idea. Can I pick your brain?"

MEANING: To get ideas or information from someone

Practice makes perfect

Band practice was underway. Zeke was working on a trumpet solo, and he was having trouble hitting the highest note.

"It's a pretty hard solo," said Mr. Sloan, the band director. "Especially that part." He grinned. "I think you already know what I'm going to tell you. . . ."

"I know, I know!" Zeke answered with a smile. "You tell us all the time. Practice makes perfect!"

MEANING: To become good at something because you do it many times

Put on the back burner

Kaitlin and her family were excited. They just bought a huge old house. It needed a lot of work, and they had a long list of projects to do. They were sitting around the kitchen table, talking about what to do first.

"I'd like to paint my room," said Kaitlin. "A very light yellow. That would look great."

"It sure would!" agreed Kaitlin's mom. "But we need to fix some of the other things first. We'll have to put painting on the back burner for a while."

MEANING: To do something later after more important things are done; to wait and do something at a later time

Rags to riches

Lara and her family loved watching the Super Singing Star show. Everyone was so talented! People who weren't famous had a chance to become stars if they won the competition.

"There's the winner from last year," said Dad.

"I remember him," Lara said. "Last year he didn't have a car, or any money. Look at him now!"

"I know," said Mom. "He's a real rags-to-riches story."

MEANING: When someone goes from being very poor to very wealthy

Rule of thumb

William was thrilled. His family just bought a big aquarium. He loved watching the fish, and he wanted to help take care of them. His mom showed him the new food they bought.

"How much do we feed them?" William asked.

"Well," said Mom, "too much food isn't good for them. As a rule of thumb, you don't give them more than they can eat right away."

MEANING: A rough guideline or measure for doing something

Second to none

Christopher's Uncle Andy had come to town for a visit. The family took Uncle Andy to his favorite seafood restaurant.

"Now," said Uncle Andy, "I would love an ice-cream cone from that wonderful little shop you took me to last time."

Soon they were all sitting at a table outside the shop, ice cream cones in their hands.

"Mmmm," said Uncle Andy, holding up his cone to admire it. "This ice cream is second to none."

MEANING: The best

The show must go on

The first performance of the school play was supposed to start in an hour. Something had gone wrong with the controls for the lights and sound. People were working to fix the problem, but nobody knew if it would be fixed in time.

"Mr. Scott," asked one of the students, "what will we do if they can't fix it? Are we still going to do the play?"

"Of course we will!" Mr. Scott replied. "It might not be perfect, but we'll do the best we can. The show must go on!"

MEANING: To follow through with an event, task, or job

Work up a head of steam

James was working in the basement. He wanted to set up a place where he could practice his guitar and drums. When his mom checked on him at noon, he was sitting in a chair, reading a magazine. When she checked again at dinnertime, everything was all set up.

"This looks great!" she told him. "I have to admit, I wondered if you could get it all done today."

"I knew I could do it," he said, grinning. "It just took me a while to work up a head of steam."

MEANING: To get energy to start on a project